Servitude Centre CIC

First published in Great Britain in 2024 by Servitude Centre CIC

ISBN 978-1-917315-00-5

Printed and bound in Great Britain by Amazon Ltd

An imprint of

Servitude Centre CIC

AF244911

To everyone, for everyone

CONTENTS

Introduction to Python

Python is a high-level, general purpose programming language that was made by Guido Van Rossum, and developed by the Python Software Foundation.

It was first released on February 20, 1991. Some popular code editors for python are Sublime Text, Visual Studio Code, Atom, and Notepad (A default editor that mainly comes with Microsoft Windows OS-powered laptops).

Instead of complex and hard to read semi-colons (';'), Python uses indentations to separate lines and determine whether there is a new line or not, so the lines don't get mixed up.

Syntax

All programming languages have a syntax. A syntax is a set of rules programming languages must follow. If there is a syntax error, the program will not work.

Replit is a software that you can use to make projects out of text-only programming languages.

You can create a program called 'Hello World'.

To do that you just need to copy the code below:

```
print("Hello World")
```

> Remember that Python is case sensitive, so do not put capital letters at the start of any line.

You can try it yourself if you want to, but you will need an IDE or code editor, such as Replit, so if you are under 13, please ask an adult to set up an account for you.

The output of the code is as followed:

Hello World

Some of the common syntax errors people make when writing the hello world code is as follows:

- Putting a capital letter for the 'print' function'.
- For getting to add speech mark.
- Not putting the close bracket.
- Putting unnecessary capital letters.

If you make a syntax error in any code editor, it will NOT run the program, and instead it will put a syntax error message on the screen.

Variables

You can make variables in Python by following the steps below.

Write the name of the variable. Then put the '=' operator. If you want to assign to a number you do not have to add speech marks, but if you are assigning it to a string (which is simply a group of words or letters), you MUST put speech marks, or there will be a syntax error (an error that makes the code un-usable).

Here are some examples:

User = "Fishoue" ✓

User = Fishoue ☒

Number = 6757 ✓

To make the screen display text and a variable, follow the steps below.

Assign the variable you want to use first.

Then on a new line, put the function 'print' then put brackets and speech marks around the text then put a comma then write the name of the variable.

For example:

User = "Fishoue"

print("Hello", User)

The output of the code above is as follows:

Hello Fishoue

You can also assign variables using arithmetic expressions by following the steps below:

Write the name of the variable then put an '=' sign. Then put a number then an arithmetic expression (* or + or – or /) then put another number after the expression.

You can put as many numbers and expressions as you want.

Here are some examples:

number = 2 * 6 + 10 – 5

count = 4 * 5 – 15 + 10 / 3

Tip: Try not to capitalize anything in python, especially the start of code, as it may result in errors and confuse you to put capitals where they are not supposed to be.

Quiz One

If you really read everything, these questions should
be really easy.

Write a script that will write 'Hello Man' without using
a variable.

____

____

Write a program that assigns a variable (it can be a number or a string) and then displays the variable.

____

____

Write a script that displays some text and a variable.

____

____

Tip: Python uses a new line for every new piece of code that makes a new output (if you look at the size of the lines carefully, you might spot something).

Operators

There are many operators that you can use to compare numbers and strings, such as -, +, *, =, ==, /, and more, but we are going to explain the basic ones.

The '-' symbol works like the normal mathematical symbol. It is a minus sign/operator, and you can use it to subtract.

For example, the code below makes the number 16:

number = 20 - 4

print(number)

The '/' operator is used for division and is unique from the usual division sign. Most programming languages to ALL of them do not use the division sign and instead use the forward slash.

This is a program that makes the number 16, the same as the above, but using a different operator and a different method:

number = 160 / 10

print(number)

The first, the '=' operator assigns what is on the right to what is on the right. Every operator uses it, other wise, they will not work.

The second, the '==' operator is a selection to check whether a variable is equal to what is on the right (a value).

These are the two operators in a script:

number = 16 (the '=' is the operator.)

if number == 16

 print(number)

The '*' operator is quite simple. It is used to times and multiply things together, for example:

number = 1.6 * 10

print(number)

The last operator, the '+', is used to add things together, for example:

number = 8 + 8

print(number)

Take the next quiz to see how much you have learnt from this section.

Quiz Two

Again, if you read everything carefully, you should be able to complete this quiz without any problems.

1. Write a script with operators to assign a variable that has the result of 190 and display it using the print function.

____

____

> You can try out all of these quizzes and activities in Replit, or another IDE or Code Editor.

2. Make a program that uses ONLY the '+' and '*' operators to generate the number 20.

____

____

3. Make notes on how to make a simple program that assigned a number to a variable and prints it.

____

____

____

____

4. Write a program that uses only the number 3, a variable called 'number', and only the '*' operator to make the number 27 and display it using the print function.

____

____

5. Make a number bigger than 100 using all of the operators you have learnt.

____

____

6. Explain how the functions and operators you have learnt work, in a few lines if possible.

____

____

____

____

____

____

____

____

Selection/Choice Management

Selection is quite simple to explain. It is choosing a choice from a range of choices and making a decision. In Python, the main selection functions are 'if', 'elif', 'else', and 'while'. This is an overview showing what each of these functions do:

The 'if' function has ONLY one choice to be chosen, and decided whether something is a specific choice, and evaluates if the choice is equal to the choice following the if statement, for example:

```
number = 16

if number = 16:

  print("This choice follows the if statement")
```

MUST DO: NEVER forget to indent the line evaluating the if statement OR you will get a syntax error.

The 'elif' statement is a combination of the words 'else' and 'if'. It is used when there are more than two options, as you can ONLY use one else statement, but you can use multiple elif statements. This elif function works exactly like the if statement.

This is an example:

number = 16

if number = 16:

  print("This follows the if statement")

elif number = 15:

  print("This statement follows the elif statement")

The else statement works like the elif statement, but you can only have one of it, for example:

number = 16

if number = 16:

  print("This follows the if statement")

elif number = 15:

  print("This statement follows the elif statement")

else:

  print("This follows the else statement")

If you looked carefully, you might have noticed a colon (':'). It is used to separate the function from the condition (what determined what evaluation should be outputted).

For the 'if' function, the colon is placed after the condition. For example:

if number = 16: (the colon is the ':' symbol)

  print("This is for the if function")

For the 'elif' function, the colon is placed after the condition, like the if function:

elif number = 16:

  print("This is for the elif function")

For the 'else' function, the colon is placed after the function (else) itself, and since 'else' is used to signify where there is no available choice, the result just follows under the statement without a condition:

else:

  print("This is for the else function")

The 'while' function works a bit differently.

It is used to continue an action as long as a condition or requirement is reached, for example:

while number == 16:

   print("This is under a while loop")

Like the elif and if functions, the colon is after the condition.

There is a second version, which checked whether a condition is failed. For example:

while number != 16

   print("This while loop will continue working until number is 16)

There is one operator that is mainly used by the while function. It is the '!=' operator. It is used to signify that a statement or condition is false, for example:

while number != 160

   print("This script is similar to the one above, except that it has the number 160, not 16)

User Input

You can use the 'input()' function and the 'int(input())' function to enter and analyse user input.

The 'input()' function is used to detect everything, especially strings, but does not calculate numbers as expected, since it will decide that the input is a string and will try to subtract a string from a string, which does not make any sense, as that is subtracting words from words. To solve this problem, the 'int(input())' is meant to subtract and add ONLY numbers. These are some examples:

This script will work as expected:

```
print("what is the current year?") ✔
answer = int(input()) ✔
```

This script is wrong and will result in a syntax error:

```
print("what is the current year?") ✔
answer = input() ☒
```

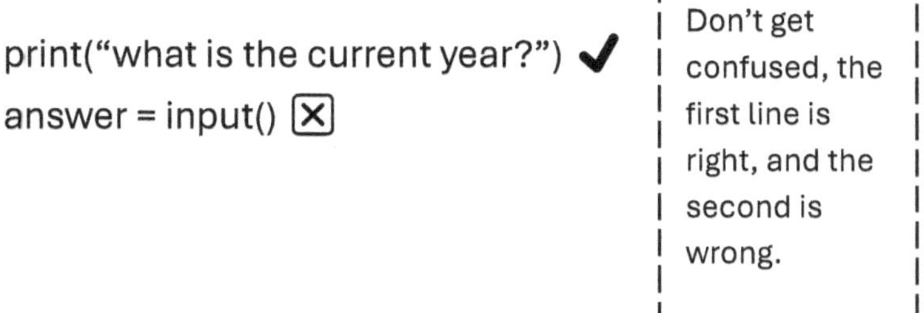

This example quiz uses the 'input()' function:

```
print("Hello. What is your name?")
name = input()
print("Hello", name)
```

The next example below uses the 'int(input())' function:

```
print("What is 5 + 5?")
answer = int(input())
if answer == 10:
  print("You are correct")
else:
  print("Your answer is wrong")
```

This is the end of this section. Take the next quiz to test your learning.

Quiz Three (Final)

1. Write some code to make a simple weather app using Python only, by using all you have learnt throughout this book.

____

____

____

____

____

____

____

____

2. Explain how to use the 'if', 'elif', and 'else' functions.

____

____

____

____

____

3. What does this code do? Tick the correct option.

number = 7 * 3 + 8

print(number)

A: It makes the number 81.

B: It makes the number 29 and prints it out.

C: It prints out the variable 'number'.

4. Explain how selection works in as much detail as possible.

____

____

____

____

____

____

____

____

____

> Tip: You can refer back to other sections of this book if you need help.

5. Make a script that runs when a condition is false.

____

____

____

____

6. Make an age calculator that calculates people's age.

Please go back to the other parts of this book if you are stuck on a question, or don't understand how something works.

____

____

____

____

____

____

Be aware that in Replit, the code will round every age to January 1, Month 1, Day 1, which causes a problem, since someone for example born in August 2024, will be said as 2024 – 2024 (or the current year) 1 when it should be 1 and a few months. If this happens, it is not your fault and is just because of extreme accuracy.

THIS IS THE END OF PYTHON PROGRAMMING FOR NEOPHYTES 1.

HOPEFULLY, YOU UNDERSTAND EVERYTHING IN THIS BOOK AND CAN NOW PUT YOUR NEW SKILLS TO PRACTICE.

Abdullah Saidu was born in 2014 and made this book with his brother (Abduddayyan Saidu) at the age of ten. They enjoy computing and have a passion for programming. Abduddayyan Saidu was born in 2016 and made this book with Abdullah saidu at the age of eight.

They are currently living in Stoke-On-Trent, UK.